TOBIAS

THE BOY WHO FACED A DEMON

Written and Illustrated by
Rhee Hahn Young
이한영

Pauline
BOOKS & MEDIA

Library of Congress Control Number: 9780819827616

ISBN 10: 0-8198-2761-4

ISBN 13: 978-0-8198-2761-6

Written and illustrated by Rhee Hahn Young

Cover design by Daughters of St. Paul

Design by 하느님의 사람 토빗 Written and Illustrated by 이한영 (Rhee Hahn Young)

Published by Pauline Books & Media, 50 Saint Paul's Avenue, Boston, MA 02130-3491

Printed in the U.S.A.

TTBWFAD VSAUSAPEOILL7-1510212 2762-2

www.pauline.org

Pauline Books & Media is the publishing house of the Daughters of St. Paul, an international congregation of women religious serving the Church with the communications media.

1 2 3 4 5 6 7 8 9 28 27 26 25 24

TOBIAS

THE BOY WHO FACED A DEMON

MY NAME IS TOBIT! I AM LEAVING THISBE RIGHT NOW AND GOING TO JERUSALEM TO OFFER SACRIFICES ACCORDING TO GOD'S WORD.
메에-
BAA
메에-
BAA

COME ON, LET'S GO.
스
SWISH
TOBIT!

JERUSALEM
와글
HEE-HAW
와글
HEE-HAW

HEY TOBIT! OVER HERE! COME GREET YOUR RELATIVES.
LONG TIME NO SEE, RAGUEL!
ARE YOU GOING TO SACRIFICE THESE ANIMALS?
YES, I'M BRINGING TO THE TEMPLE THE SHEEP THAT WERE BORN THIS YEAR.
메에 -
HMMM
EVER SINCE THE TRIBE OF OUR ANCESTOR NAPHTALI SEPARATED ITSELF FROM JERUSALEM, ALL OUR RELATIVES HAVE BEEN OFFERING SACRIFICES ON THE MOUNTAINS OF GALILEE.

THEY SHOULD BE OFFERED HERE IN JERUSALEM.
THE RUMOR WAS CORRECT! TOBIT IS A ROLE MODEL FOR OUR RELATIVES.
쉬익
WINK
I AM JUST FOLLOWING THE TEACHINGS OF OUR FAITH.
I JUST CAME TO ENJOY THE FESTIVAL WITH SOME FRIENDS . . .
BUT I WILL COME WITH YOU WHEN YOU GO TO OFFER THE SACRIFICE.
THANK YOU!
OH YEAH, HOW IS YOUR GRANDMA?

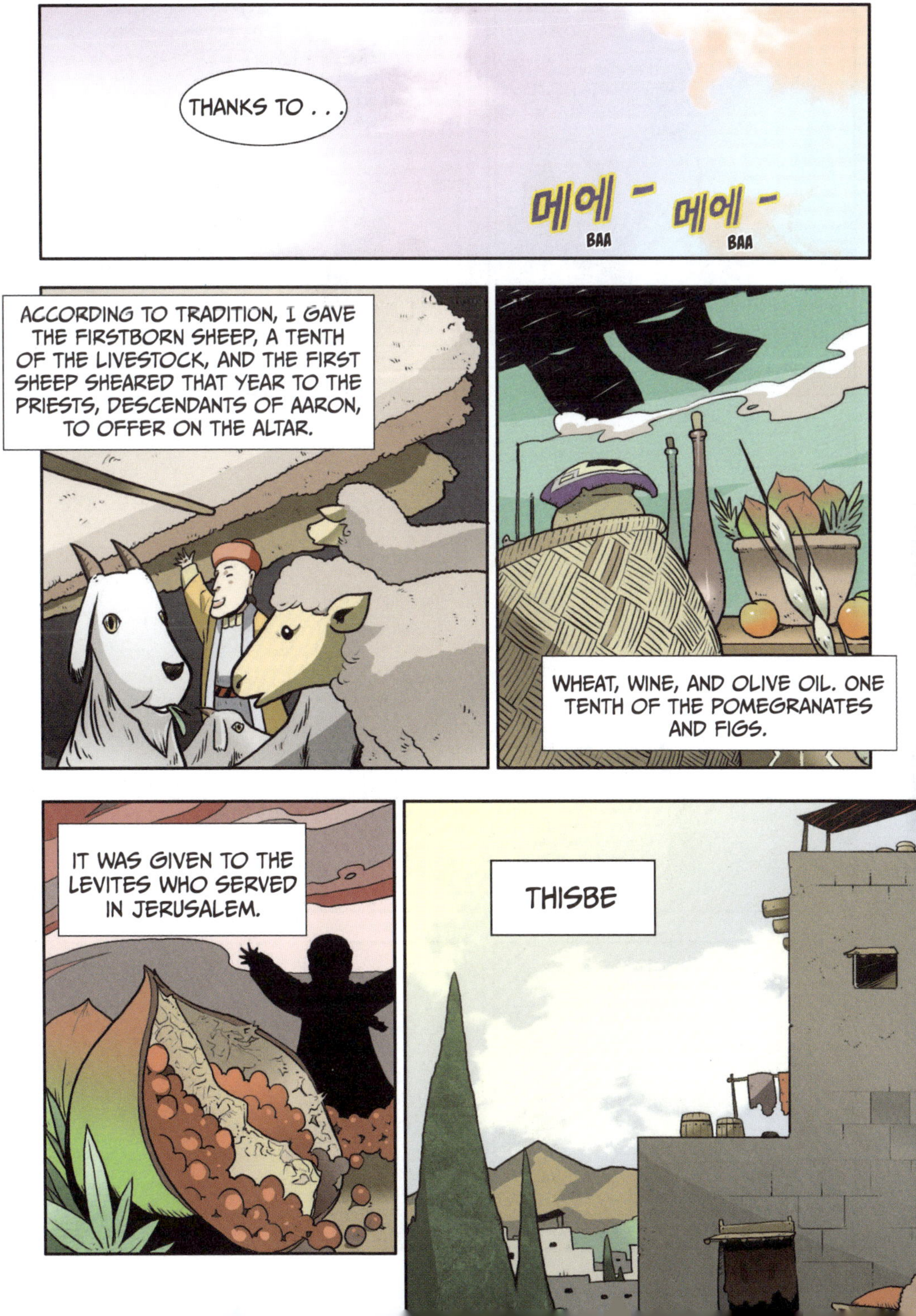
THANKS TO . . .
메에 - 메에 -
BAA BAA
ACCORDING TO TRADITION, I GAVE THE FIRSTBORN SHEEP, A TENTH OF THE LIVESTOCK, AND THE FIRST SHEEP SHEARED THAT YEAR TO THE PRIESTS, DESCENDANTS OF AARON, TO OFFER ON THE ALTAR.
WHEAT, WINE, AND OLIVE OIL. ONE TENTH OF THE POMEGRANATES AND FIGS.
IT WAS GIVEN TO THE LEVITES WHO SERVED IN JERUSALEM.
THISBE

YOU ARE ALREADY BACK FROM JERUSALEM?
HANIEL!
MY DEAR, YOU WILL TRULY POSSESS THE LOVE OF GOD!
AHIKAR HAS GROWN SO MUCH.
하핫
HAHA
HE'S SO IMMERSED IN HIS STUDIES THESE DAYS, HE'S BECOME SKINNY.
HE MUST BE A GENIUS!
OH DAD!

TOBIT!
YOU SENT FOOD TO MY CHILD.
HOW CAN I EVER THANK YOU . . .
I WAS JUST FOLLOWING GOD'S WORD.
MAY GOD'S GRACE BE WITH YOU.
. . .

I'M BACK, GRANDMA!
GOOD JOB, TOBIT . . .
I HAVE SOMETHING TO TELL YOU. I WAS WAITING FOR YOU.
ARE YOU WORRIED ABOUT SOMETHING?
IT WAS DIFFICULT FOR YOU WHEN YOUR PARENTS DIED, BUT YOU HAVE GROWN UP WELL WITH GOD'S GRACE.

* AT THAT TIME IT WAS CUSTOMARY TO MARRY WITHIN ONE'S EXTENDED FAMILY OR CLAN.

두근 두근
BA-DUM
BA-DUM
MY WIFE IS THE BEAUTIFUL AND WISE ANNA!
WAH WAH!
WHAT SHOULD WE NAME OUR BABY?
MY FATHER IS TOBIEL, I AM TOBIT, THEN . . .

THIS GUY SHOULD BE NAMED TOBIAS.
BUT THIS HAPPINESS DIDN'T LAST LONG.
AHHH!
SLICE
슈아악
NO!
THUD
털썩
AHH!
와!
SCHWING
THE ASSYRIANS!
THE ASSYRIANS ARE INVADING!
으악!
WHACK
까!
CRACK

MY PEOPLE WERE HELPLESS . . .
MY FAMILY AND I WERE TAKEN CAPTIVE.
CHEER UP, HONEY . . .
WHY IS LIFE SUCH AN ORDEAL FOR US . . .

WHAT NOW?
GOD WILL NOT FORSAKE US.
TOBIT, HAVE YOU BEEN CAPTURED TOO?!
RAGUEL, YOU'RE ALIVE!
덥석!
GRASP!
WHERE ARE THEY TAKING US?
I DON'T KNOW.
IT SEEMS THAT WE'VE ALREADY ENTERED THE LAND OF THE ASSYRIANS.
헉 헉
PANT PANT

헉헉헉
HUFF WHEEZE
!
비틀
DIZZY
HONEY!
척
PLOP
SORRY. I AM SO THIRSTY.
MY POOR WIFE! HOW CAN I PROVIDE FOR HER?
TAKE THIS WATER.

THEN WHAT ARE YOU GOING TO DO?!
IT'S OKAY!
I'LL SHARE WITH MY WIFE. JUST HANG IN THERE!
MY RELATIVE RAGUEL FELL BEHIND AND WAS EXILED ELSEWHERE.
AND FINALLY, WHERE HAD WE ARRIVED?

IT WAS NINEVEH, THE LAND OF THE ASSYRIANS.
WE HAVE BEEN EXILED TO THE CAPITAL CITY OF ASSYRIA!
THERE IS NO ESCAPE NOW!
....

WE SETTLED HERE AND STARTED MAKING A NEW HOME.
I'M BACK!
WELCOME! ANOTHER HARD DAY AT WORK?
철컥
CREAK
EASIER WORK IS A LUXURY WE CAN'T AFFORD.
슥 슥
SWISH
FORTUNATELY, WE'RE HAVING LAMB FOR DINNER.
OH! WHERE DID YOU GET THAT!?

IT'S DIFFICULT TO EAT OUR TRADITIONAL FOODS THESE DAYS . . .
BECAUSE IT'S HARD TO FIND THE INGREDIENTS.
OUR RELATIVES SEEM TO HAVE ADAPTED TO THE FOOD HERE. WE COULD ALSO . . .
WHAT!?
WE MUST NOT EAT THE FOOD OF THE STRANGERS HERE!
BUT IF THINGS CONTINUE, THERE WILL BE NOTHING TO EAT!

WE CAN'T LET TOBIAS GROW UP NOT KNOWING WHO WE ARE AND WHERE WE CAME FROM!
아♪
MMM
냠 냠
YUM
AND . . .
I KNOW, I KNOW! WE ALSO CAN'T FORGET GOD.
THE NEXT DAY
뚝닥
뚝닥
BANG BANG
HEY, TOBIT!
뚝따닥 -
THUD
뚝닥
THUD
HEY, TOBIT!

HANIEL, WHAT'S GOING ON?
I CAME TO OFFER YOU A GOOD OPPORTUNITY.
OUR AHIKAR GOT AN OFFICIAL POSITION IN THE PALACE.
흐흐흐
HEHEHE
CONGRATULATIONS, WHAT A BRIGHT KID!
SO I HAVE BEEN TOLD HE COULD GIVE YOU A DECENT JOB!
REALLY! COULD IT BE?
SO GO TO THE PALACE TOMORROW AND SEE AHIKAR!

THIS IS THE PALACE WHERE KING SHALMANESER LIVES!
I HOPE MY JOB IS SOMETHING PLEASING TO GOD.
꼬륵
GROWL
GROWL
뒤적 뒤적
RUSTLE RUSTLE
YOU MUST BE HUNGRY. LET'S SEE, I HAD A PIECE OF BREAD . . .
탁
SNATCH
쩝쩝
MUNCH MUNCH
OH, WOW!

THANK YOU SO MUCH!
THE BREAD IS NOT MINE, BUT GOD'S. THANK GOD.
WHAT'S THIS! A BEGGAR GIVING A BEGGAR SOMETHING TO EAT!!
EEK, THE KING IS ENTERING THE PALACE. I SHOULD GET INSIDE.
AHIKAR!
UNCLE TOBIT!
WELCOME! MY FATHER SPOKE TO ME.
THANKS FOR THIS. WHAT IS THE JOB?

OH, I'M STILL AT THE LOWEST LEVEL. I THINK MY FATHER GOT AHEAD OF HIMSELF.
I UNDERSTAND!
DID I SPEAK WITH ANNA TOO QUICKLY? SHE'LL BE DISAPPOINTED AGAIN . . .
DO YOU NEED A JOB?
IT'S THE KING!
넙죽!
THUD
YOU DON'T LOOK GREEDY.
쿵-
BOW

HAS HE BEEN WATCHING ME?
I HAVE A JOB FOR SOMEONE WHO ISN'T GREEDY.
GOOD LUCK!
불-!
RISE!
WHY AREN'T YOU FOLLOWING?
COMING!
WAS IT GOD'S HELP? HE CAUGHT THE EYE OF KING SHALMANESER AND WON HIS FAVOR.
ALRIGHT, THAT'S GREAT!
MISSION COMPLETE!
?
뾰옹~
HUH

SO THE KING GAVE ME THE JOB OF BUYING ALL THE GOODS HE NEEDED.
THE LAST GUY LOST HIS HEAD BECAUSE HE EMBEZZLED.
끽
SLICE
DO WELL!
꿀꺽
GULP
HEY, WELL DONE!
와
WOW
WHAT A RELIEF.
MY PEOPLE REJOICED AS IF IT WAS THEIR OWN JOY.
WHEN I COULD AFFORD IT, I BEGAN TO BE MORE CHARITABLE AND GIVE ALMS TO MY RELATIVES AND OUR PEOPLE.
HIM TOO . . .
WELL, THAT WOULD BE FINE . . .
NOW EVERYONE CAN EAT!
FOOD FOR THE HUNGRY!
CLOTHES FOR THE NAKED!
I CAN'T LIVE LIKE THIS!

I USED TO GO TO MEDIA TO BUY SUPPLIES FOR THE KING. THEN ONE DAY . . .
!
NO, THIS PERSON IS . . . !
WHY WAS ONE OF MY PEOPLE LEFT DEAD LIKE THIS?
I COULDN'T GET PAST IT.
THAT'S THE WAY THAT IT IS.
TSK TSK

BY THE WAY, IF YOU GET CAUGHT HANDLING A CORPSE LIKE THAT, THE KILLER MIGHT TAKE REVENGE ON YOU!
WHAT ARE YOU TALKING ABOUT! OUR PEOPLE ARE MADE OF EARTH, SO WE MUST BE BURIED IN THE SOIL.
THAT'S GOD'S WILL.
IT'S A SAD REALITY THAT WE ARE LOOKED DOWN ON BECAUSE WE ARE FROM AN EXILED NATION.
흐윽 흐윽
SOB
I'M NOT GOING TO AVOID DOING IT WHEN NECESSARY!
. . . .
ALTHOUGH THE HEARTBREAKING EXILE CONTINUED,
MY WEALTH INCREASED.

RHAGES IN MEDIA
TOBIT, THIS DEAL WENT WELL!
GERSHON, YOU HAVE BEEN FAITHFUL ALL THESE YEARS.
BUT THEY SAY THAT THE NUMBER OF THIEVES HAS GREATLY INCREASED BETWEEN MEDIA AND NINEVEH THESE DAYS . . .
AND I'M ABOUT TO GO BACK WITH TEN TALENTS OF SILVER!
SINCE YOU COME TO MEDIA OFTEN, WHY DON'T YOU LEAVE IT WITH GERSHON?
WHAT ARE YOU SAYING?

I KNOW GERSHON'S CHARACTER WELL. HE WOULD NEVER TOUCH OTHER PEOPLE'S MONEY.
YES, I TRUST GERSHON, TOO!
OKAY, I'LL WRITE UP A CERTIFICATE BEFORE THE TWO OF YOU.
TEN TALENTS OF SILVER WAS A LARGE SUM OF MONEY, BUT WE DID NOT NEED IT URGENTLY ENOUGH TO RISK IT.
BY THE WAY . . .
KING SHALMANESER IS DEAD!
후후후~
HEH HEHEH
I HEARD YOU BECAME THE KING'S TREASURER?
SHALMANESER'S SON SENNACHERIB BECAME KING.

JUST TREASURER? HE'S AN ADMINISTRATOR AND HE'S ALSO IN CHARGE OF THE SEAL!
HEY, THAT'S GREAT!
I WAS LUCKY.
HOWEVER, THE KING'S HEART IS NASTY . . .
FATHER!
쉬~
SHHH
SIGH, I HAVE TO WATCH MY MOUTH!
IT WAS RIGHT WHEN SENNACHERIB BECAME KING THAT MANY PROBLEMS AROSE.
AS WARS BECAME MORE FREQUENT, THE NUMBER OF THIEVES INCREASED,
SO MEDIA WAS COMPLETELY BLOCKED OFF.

SO YOU CAN'T MAKE IT TO MEDIA NOW?
YES, THE KING HAS ALSO SAID NOT TO DO BUSINESS WITH MEDIA FOR THE TIME BEING.
MY FRIENDS SAY THAT SENNACHERIB IS A BAD RULER.
HE IS A MAN WHO DEFIES THE WILL OF GOD. SOMEDAY HE WILL BE JUDGED.
YOU SAY THEY ARE ATTACKING OUR HOMELAND?
DO YOU WONDER HOW WELL OUR PEOPLE ARE FIGHTING?
SENNACHERIB INVADED JUDAH AND ATTACKED JERUSALEM.
SENNACHERIB'S SERVANTS SHOUTED AT THE PEOPLE ABOVE THE WALLS OF JERUSALEM TO SURRENDER.

THEN KING HEZEKIAH PRAYED TOWARD HEAVEN.
AN ANGEL SENT BY THE LORD APPEARED THROUGH THE CLOUDS.
IT IS SAID THAT THEY DEFEATED THE ARMY OF KING SENNACHERIB.
BUT SENNACHERIB GOT AWAY?
THAT'S RIGHT. YOU SHOULDN'T TELL OTHER PEOPLE ABOUT THIS.
I KNOW.
IF YOU TALK LIKE THAT, THEY'LL KILL YOU AND DUMP YOU OUTSIDE THE CASTLE, RIGHT?

DO YOU KIDS TALK ABOUT THIS?
YES . . .
TODAY NATAL'S FATHER WAS ALSO KILLED AND ABANDONED OUTSIDE THE CASTLE.
WHAT!
벌떡
RISE!
HONEY, YOU CAN'T GO OUT!
덜컥
CREAK
WE MUST BURY OUR OWN PEOPLE!
IF YOU GET CAUGHT, YOU'LL DIE!
I'M TRYING TO DO THE RIGHT THING!
꽉!
CLENCH

THIS, THIS . . .
THIS STRANGE WOUND ON MY FACE ISN'T HEALING!
긁적긁적
SCRATCH SCRATCH
FATHER, CALM DOWN.
SHUT UP! IT'S ALL BECAUSE OF THE ISRAELITES!
IF YOU GET ANGRY, YOUR WOUNDS WILL GET WORSE.
UGH, I CAN'T POSSIBLY FORGIVE THEM!
HEY! WASN'T THERE AN ISRAELI WHO MOCKED ME TODAY? GO FIND HIM!
DIDN'T YOU ALREADY KILL HIM?

DEAD OR NOT, I'LL HAVE TO KILL HIM SEVERAL MORE TIMES TO FEEL BETTER.
찌릿
GLARE
다다다닷
THUMP THUMP
YES, I'M GOING!
THIS IS NOT THE TIME. YOU MUST TAKE CARE OF THE COUNTRY!
HOW LONG WILL YOU MAKE THE PEOPLE SUFFER?
HOW DARE YOU GIVE ME ADVICE!
버럭!
ARRRR
YOU TWO, TAKE A CLUB BATH RIGHT NOW!
?!

저벅
저벅
TRUDGE TRUDGE
...
HONEY!
SENNACHERIB ORDERED THE BODY OF NATAL'S FATHER TO BE FOUND.

!
AHIKAR SAYS SOMEONE SAW YOU BURY HIM!
WHAT ARE YOU DOING, RUN AWAY!
터억-!
SHOVE
ANNA . . .
DON'T DIE. IF YOU LIVE, GOD WILL HELP YOU.

타다닷-
THUMP THUMP
SENNACHERIB WOULD TAKE EVERYTHING I OWNED, SO I PRAYED THAT AT LEAST MY FAMILY WOULD SURVIVE.
탁 탁
THUMP THUMP
PRAYER WAS ALL I COULD DO.
I LOST EVERYTHING.

두리번 두리번
TREMBLE TREMBLE
SWISH
BROTHERS!
ESARHADDON!
깜짝
GASP!
WHAT'S THE MATTER? WHY ARE YOU COMING OUT OF MY FATHER'S BEDROOM AT THIS LATE HOUR?
IT'S THAT . . .
. . . !

THIS, THIS WAS FOR THE PEOPLE.
LET US GO, ESARHADDON!
WHAT? NO WAY! FATHER!
휘익
WHIRL
타-앗!
AHHHHH!
OH, HOW CAN THIS BE . . . !
BECOME THE KING AND MAKE GOOD DECISIONS!
!

THE TWO PRINCES FLED TO MOUNT ARARAT.
KING ESARHADDON ASCENDED TO THE THRONE.
THIS WAS ABOUT 40 DAYS AFTER I STARTED RUNNING AWAY.
AHIKAR! I WANT TO ENTRUST ADMINISTRATION AND FINANCES TO YOU AGAIN. WOULD YOU DO THIS?
YES, BUT I HAVE ONE REQUEST.
. . . !
OK, TELL ME.

AMONG OUR PEOPLE, THERE IS A PERSON WHO IS RUNNING AWAY BECAUSE HE WAS HATED BY THE PREVIOUS KING.
A MAN NAMED TOBIT . . .
PLEASE FORGIVE HIS WRONGS IF EVEN JUST TO APPEASE THE PUBLIC SENTIMENT.
THE PEOPLE OF ISRAEL WILL THANK YOU FOR YOUR CONSIDERATION.
GOOD!
HOWEVER, CONSIDERING HIS GUILT, HIS PROPERTY AND TITLE CANNOT BE RETURNED.
척!
POINT!

터벅
TRUDGE
터벅
TRUDGE
FATHER!
멍
멍
WOOF
WOOF
TOBY!

HONEY!
THANK GOD WE ARE ALL SAFE!
WELCOME BACK! WE ALL GATHERED FOOD LITTLE BY LITTLE AND PREPARED A FEAST TO CELEBRATE.
. . .
. . . TOBY, COME HERE!

THE FOOD IS PLENTIFUL. GO OUT NOW AND BRING IN AS MANY POOR PEOPLE AS YOU SEE AMONG OUR PEOPLE.
I WANT TO BE WITH THEM. WE WILL WAIT UNTIL YOU COME BACK.
AS ALWAYS, YES!
COME! KALEV!
타닥
THUMP THUMP
HOW'S THE NEW RULER?

MUCH BETTER THAN SENNACHERIB!
HE SEEMS TO KNOW TO BE AFRAID OF PUBLIC OPINION!
I HOPE HE DOESN'T LOOK DOWN ON OUR PEOPLE NOW . . .
BY THE WAY, SINCE YOU HAVE NEITHER WEALTH NOR WORK NOW, HURRY UP AND GET YOUR HEALTH BACK AND FIND WORK.
척
STOMP
TOBY!
WHY DID YOU COME BACK ALONE?

ONE OF OUR OWN PEOPLE WAS STRANGLED AND HIS BODY THROWN IN THE MARKETPLACE.
WHAT?!
NO ONE EVEN NOTICES HIM!
벌떡
RISE
!
OH NO, THIS GUY! . . . NOT TODAY!
TOBIT, LOOK! STOP MEDDLING!

BURYING THAT KINSMAN'S BODY AND GOING THROUGH THAT HARDSHIP . . .
TSSK TSSK . . .

SHAKE
...

YES, NOW WE CAN BEGIN.
TREMBLE
...

FATHER . . . ?!
!

IT LOOKS LIKE FATHER WENT TO BURY THE BODY LAST NIGHT.
I SHOULD COVER YOU WITH A BLANKET.
SWOOSH
PLOP

AHHHHHHHHH!
FATHER!
EWWW!

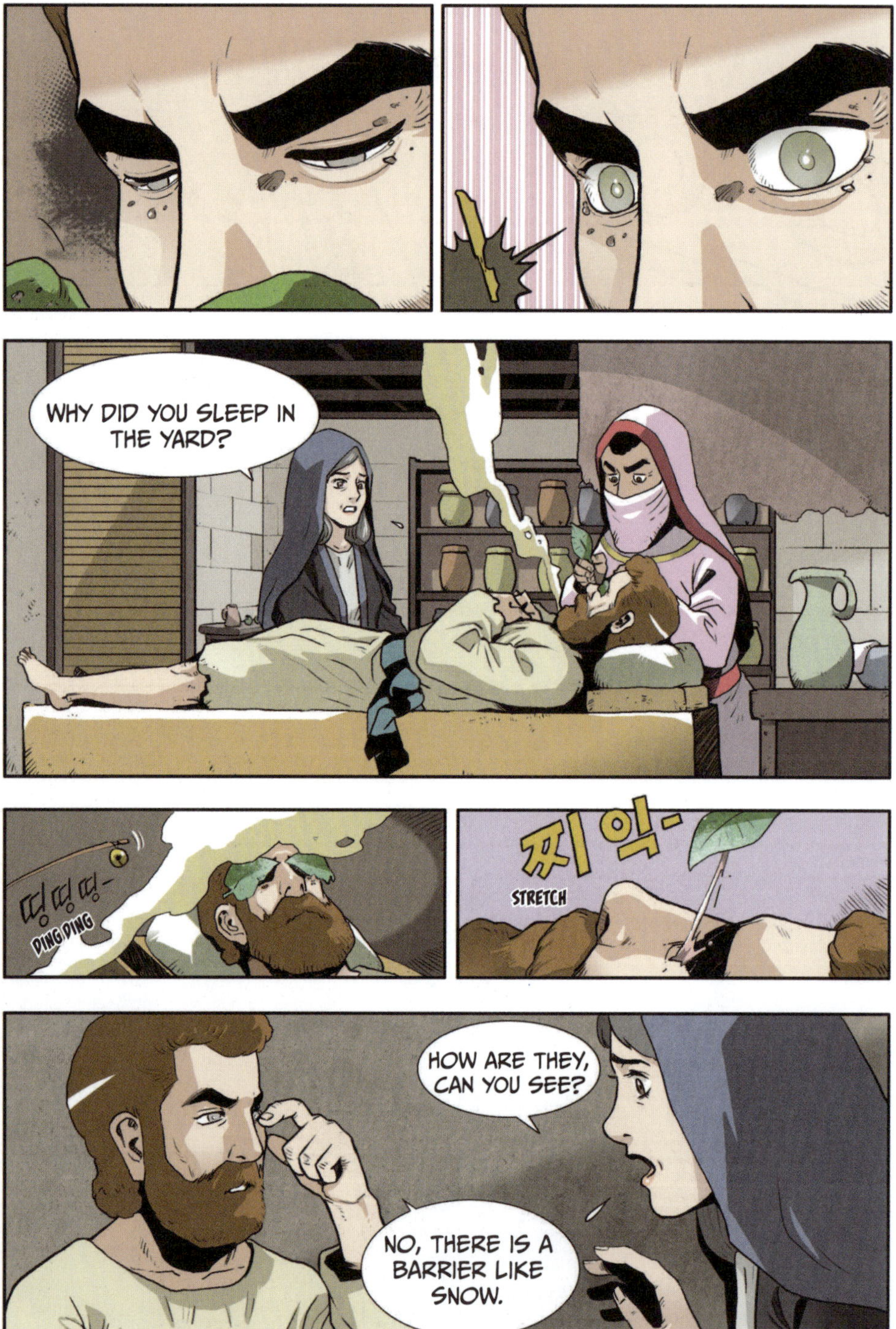
WHY DID YOU SLEEP IN THE YARD?
띵 띵 띵-
DING DING
찌익-
STRETCH
HOW ARE THEY, CAN YOU SEE?
NO, THERE IS A BARRIER LIKE SNOW.

IT LOOKS LIKE THE POISON SPREAD.
I HAVE NO CLUE.
...!
SOON ENOUGH, WITH HIS VISION GONE, PEOPLE WHISPERED THAT IT WAS BECAUSE THE DEAD SENNACHERIB HAD PUT A CURSE ON HIM.

MANY YEARS PASSED.
MEDIA, ECBATANA
HONEY, HAS THE GROOM GONE UP?
YES, NOTHING SHOULD HAPPEN.
SIGH
CLANK
THIS TIME THE GROOM IS FAMOUS FOR HIS LUCK.

딸꾹
HICCUP
끼이-
HICCUP
WHERE'S MY BRIDE?
비틀 비틀
STAGGER
YOU ARE SO BEAUTIFUL.
스윽
DIZZY

BUT THEY SAY THAT EVERYONE WHO MARRIES YOU DIES BEFORE THEY GO TO SLEEP.
AREN'T YOU AFRAID?
IT'S A CHANCE TO WIN A BEAUTIFUL BRIDE. I DON'T BELIEVE IN SUPERSTITION!
BESIDES, THE FATHER-IN-LAW IS ALSO RICH. WHOOPEE!
스르르
SWIRL
HAHAHA
YOU FOOL! ONE MORE PREY!

슈-
GROWL
크아아아아-
WOOOSH

짹 짹
TWEET TWEET
똑똑똑
KNOCK KNOCK
YOUR MOTHER SENT ME.
. . .

WHAT . . . !?
휙
TOSS
GET OUT! I MEAN IT, GET OUT!
THUNK
UGH!
IS IT MY FAULT YOUR HUSBANDS DIED? WHY ARE YOU TAKING YOUR ANGER OUT ON ME?
IF YOU WANT TO RESENT SOMEONE, BLAME YOURSELF!
RAGUEL! I CAN'T BELIEVE THIS. AGAIN . . .
HIM TOO!
웅성웅성
HOW MANY TIMES HAS THIS HAPPENED ALREADY?
THERE MUST BE AN EVIL SPIRIT!

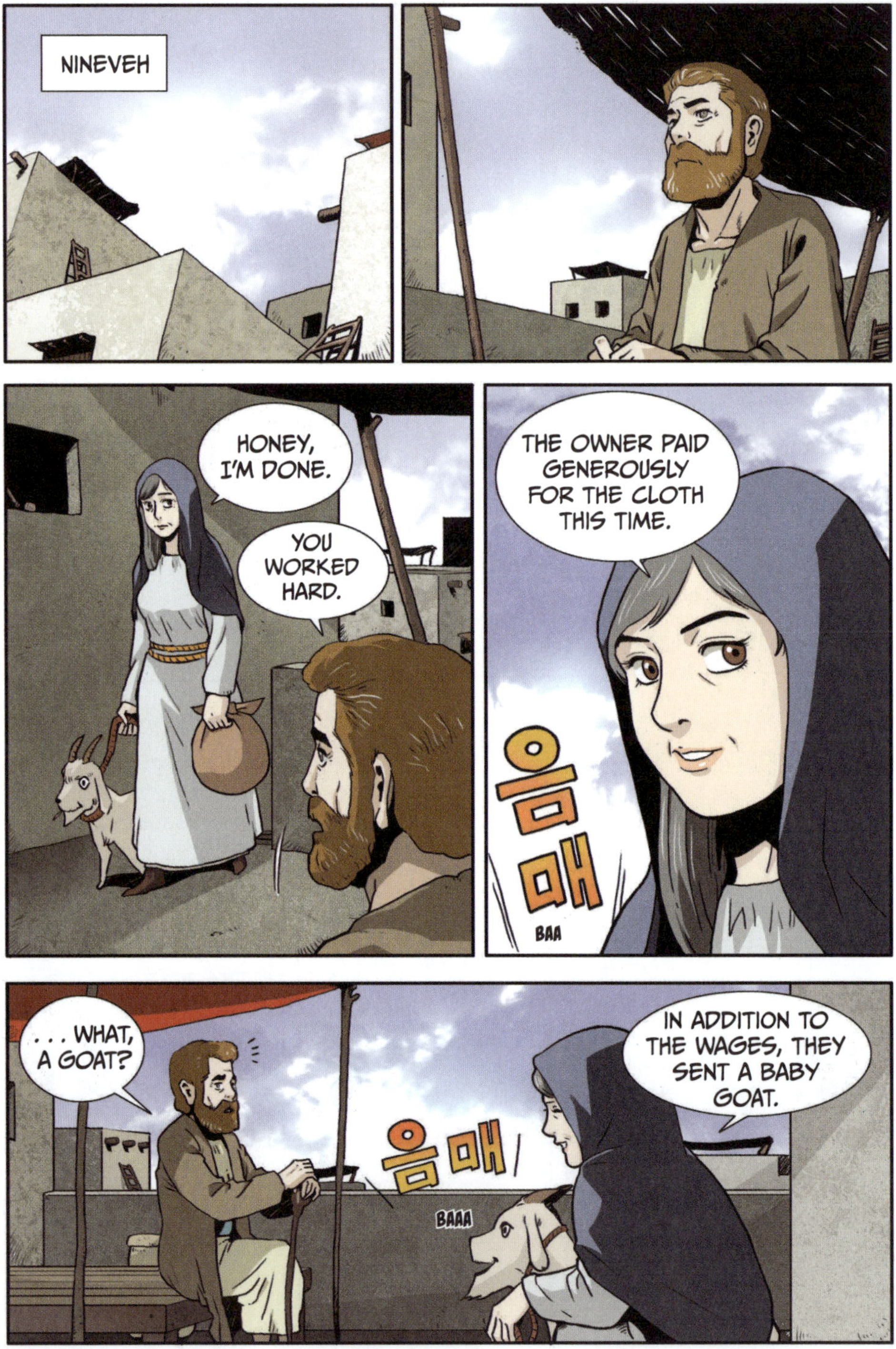
NINEVEH
HONEY, I'M DONE.
YOU WORKED HARD.
THE OWNER PAID GENEROUSLY FOR THE CLOTH THIS TIME.
음매
BAA
. . . WHAT, A GOAT?
IN ADDITION TO THE WAGES, THEY SENT A BABY GOAT.
음매
BAAA

GIVE IT BACK!
HUMPH
HONEY!
YOU STOLE THE GOAT, DIDN'T YOU?
WHAT, WHAT?
LOOK AT YOU! YOU THINK I WOULD STEAL?
ARE YOU IN A POSITION TO TALK LIKE THAT?
AH, ANNA!
ARE YOU SAYING OUR POVERTY IS MY FAULT?
YES, WHAT DID YOU GAIN FROM YOUR ALMS? WHAT WAS THE PRICE OF GOOD DEEDS?
YOU LIVE WITH PEOPLE POINTING AT YOU!

I'M REALLY SICK OF THIS NOW . . . !
AHH . . . !
비틀
STAGGER
비틀
STAGGER
FATHER . . . !
털썩
CRASH!
MEANWHILE IN RAGUEL'S HOUSE IN ECBATANA
IS THERE ANY REASON I SHOULD LIVE ANY LONGER?

IF I KILL MYSELF . . .
MY FATHER WILL BE HUMILIATED EVEN MORE!
AH! LORD, WHAT SHOULD I DO?
MERCIFUL GOD! PLEASE HELP ME ESCAPE THIS EVIL SPIRIT!
MY PARENTS ARE SO ASHAMED. PLEASE FREE THEM FROM THIS PAIN! GOD, HAVE MERCY ON ME.
!!!

OH LORD! YOU ARE THE JUDGE OF THIS WORLD, AND YOUR VERDICT IS TRUE.
BECAUSE OUR PEOPLE SINNED AGAINST YOU, YOU SENT THEM INTO EXILE AND MADE THEM A MOCKERY.
BUT NOW I CAN NO LONGER BEAR MY PUNISHMENT. I AM A BURDEN TO MY FAMILY.
SOB
I DON'T WANT TO LIVE ANY LONGER.
...

PLEASE, PLEASE TAKE ME.

쿠우우우
SWOOSH
RAPHAEL!
YES?
DO YOU REMEMBER THE ONE YOU HELPED LAST TIME?

WASN'T IT TOBIT?
RIGHT, AND THERE IS A GIRL NAMED SARAH.
HMM
TOBIT AND SARAH.
YES, I WOULD LIKE TO SEND YOU FOR THEIR SAKE.
YES!
척!
BOW
JUST GIVE ME THE ORDER.

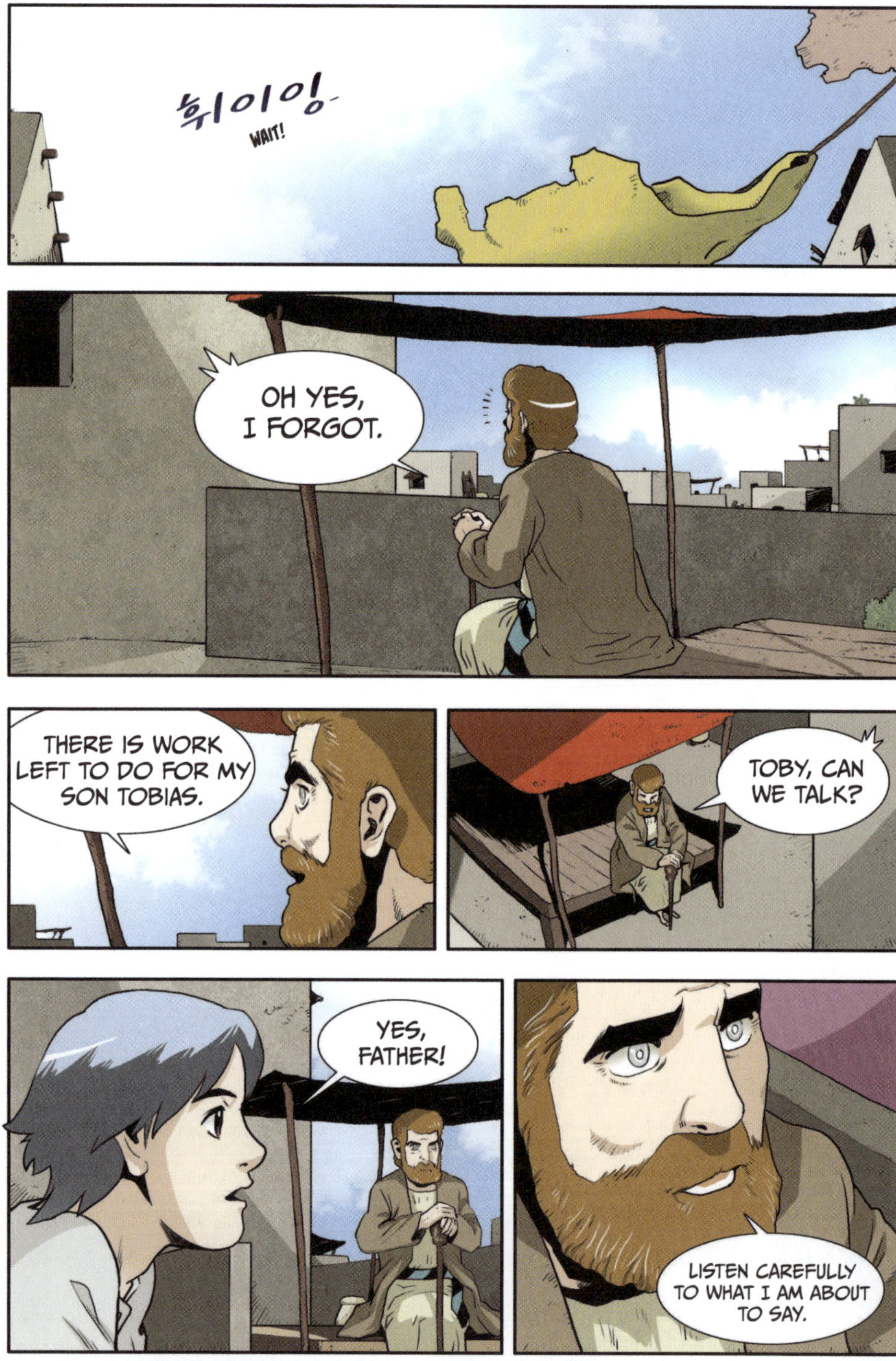
휘이잉
WAIT!
OH YES, I FORGOT.
THERE IS WORK LEFT TO DO FOR MY SON TOBIAS.
TOBY, CAN WE TALK?
YES, FATHER!
LISTEN CAREFULLY TO WHAT I AM ABOUT TO SAY.

I BEGGED GOD TO DIE. BURY YOUR FATHER WELL!
FATHER!
YOU MUST NEVER FORGET THAT YOUR MOTHER LOVES YOU.
WHEN YOUR MOTHER DIES, BURY HER IN THE SAME GRAVE WITH ME!
DON'T TALK LIKE THAT!
훌쩍
SOB!
I HELPED ANYONE WHO NEEDED IT.
YOU SHOULD TOO. WHEN YOU GIVE, IT PLEASES HIM.
YOU MEAN GOD?
YES!
DON'T BE DISCOURAGED THAT WE HAVE BECOME POOR. IT IS GOD'S WILL.
YES . . .

YOU'RE TALKING ABOUT GOD AGAIN!
LISTEN CAREFULLY, FROM NOW ON YOU . . .
YOU WILL GO TO RHAGES IN MEDIA.
깜짝-!
GASP!
WHAT?
RHAGES OF MEDIA?
슈우우우
SWOOOSH

NOW, WHAT KIND OF PERSON WILL GOD CHANGE ME INTO THIS TIME?
WELL . . .
I WILL NEED TO LOOK LIKE ONE OF THEIR KINSMEN.
피이-잉
FWISH!
ALRIGHT, THANKS BE TO GOD!
팟!
SWIRL!

IS THIS THE DEED?
YES, IT HAS ALREADY BEEN SEVERAL YEARS SINCE I ENTRUSTED IT TO GERSHON.
TEN TALENTS OF SILVER? WHOA!
부르르
TREMBLE
THE ROAD TO RHAGES WILL NOT BE EASY.
GO AHEAD AND FIND A GUIDE YOU CAN TRUST.

ARE MY FATHER'S WORDS TRUE?
IT WOULD BE GREAT, BUT WHERE AM I SUDDENLY GOING TO FIND A GUIDE?
콰ㅇ
POW
OUCH, SORRY.
투둑
CRACK
THE PRECIOUS BRACELET I BOUGHT IN MEDIA IS BROKEN.

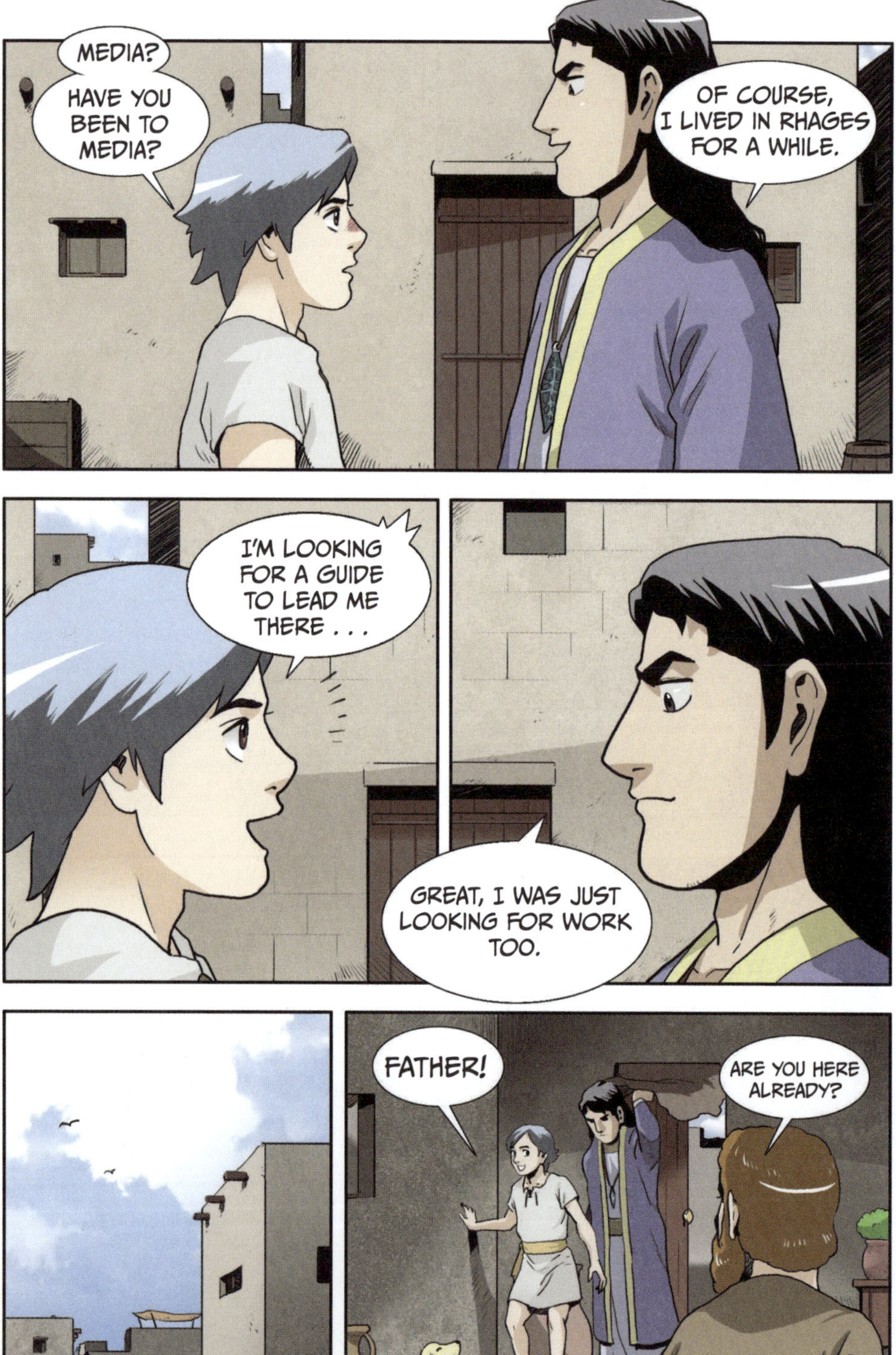
MEDIA?
HAVE YOU BEEN TO MEDIA?
OF COURSE, I LIVED IN RHAGES FOR A WHILE.
I'M LOOKING FOR A GUIDE TO LEAD ME THERE . . .
GREAT, I WAS JUST LOOKING FOR WORK TOO.
FATHER!
ARE YOU HERE ALREADY?

YES, I WAS LUCKY TO FIND ONE OF OUR PEOPLE.
THAT'S GREAT. I HAVE TO GET TO KNOW HIM MYSELF!
COME HERE, YOUNG MAN!
MAY YOUR JOY BE FULL!
꾸벅
NOD
HOW CAN I REJOICE, WHEN I CAN'T EVEN SEE THE LIGHT OF THE SKY?
BE BRAVE. GOD WILL HEAL YOU SOON.
THANK YOU.
BUT WHAT KIND OF FAMILY ARE YOU FROM?

I AM AZARIAH SON OF HANANIAH.
피웅-
SWISH
HANANIAH?
OH, THAT'S RIGHT!
YOUR RELATIVES AND I KNOW EACH OTHER WELL. I AM EMBARRASSED I ASKED.
I UNDERSTAND. YOU'RE ENTRUSTING ME WITH AN IMPORTANT JOB AS A GUIDE.
FOR YOUR WAGES, THIS WILL DO.
WHEN YOU COME BACK, I WILL GIVE YOU MORE.

DON'T WORRY, HE WILL COME BACK SAFE AND SOUND.
MAY GOD BE WITH YOU.
THERE COULD STILL BE MANY THIEVES. HOW CAN WE SEND OUR PRECIOUS SON LIKE THAT!?
DON'T WORRY. IT SEEMS THAT WE ARE TOO ACCUSTOMED TO MISFORTUNE.
멍멍-
WOOF WOOF
KALEV! COME WITH ME!

TOBY . . . !
WE CAN JUST KEEP LIVING A HARD LIFE. LET'S NOT BE GREEDY. PLEASE?
TOBIAS HAS EVERYTHING HE NEEDS NOW, AND SOMEHOW I FEEL THAT THE LORD WILL BE WITH ME.
. . . .
TOBY, YOU CAN CALL ME BROTHER.
OKAY, BROTHER!

HAVE YOU EVER LEFT THE HOUSE?
PANT 헥헥 PANT
우~~ WHEEZE
NOPE . . .
HEY, LET'S STAY TOGETHER. YOU'RE WALKING TOO FAST!
IT'S ONLY YOUR FIRST DAY, AND YOU ALREADY LOOK EXHAUSTED.
UNLIKE MY BROTHER, I HAVE NEVER LEFT THE CITY.
WHOA, YOU'RE WEAKER THAN YOU LOOK.
LET'S REST OVER THAT HILL.

GASP!
SERIOUSLY, IF WE ARE DELAYED LIKE THIS FROM THE START, WHEN WILL YOU GET BACK HOME?
MAYBE I CAN'T KEEP UP WITH YOU . . . GASP . . . !
YOU MUST BE STRONG THROUGH THIS TRIP AND GROW UP.
. . . .

UGH! DRINKING WATER LIKE THIS IS BOUND TO MAKE YOU TIRED!
NO MATTER HOW MUCH WATER I DRINK, I AM ALWAYS THIRSTY. WHAT SHOULD I DO?
IT IS LIKE HUMAN GREED: NO MATTER HOW MUCH YOU HAVE, YOU WANT MORE!
THE TIGRIS RIVER!

WOW, WATER!
타다다
DASH
NOW I FEEL ALIVE!
!
OH!
츄우우!

콱
CHOMP
WHAT A BIG FISH!
첨벙
SPLASH
UGH, FISH, LET ME GO!
TOBY!
AZARIAH, SON OF HANANIAH ALREADY CONSIDERS ME A WEAKLING . . .
NOW I'M BEING BELITTLED BY A FISH!
꽉
GRAB

THE FISH?!
첨벙!
SPLASH!
TOBIAS, YOU MUST CATCH THAT FISH!
끄응
WHINE
!
GOT IT!
멍멍멍
WOOF WOOF
HOW ABOUT HAVING THIS FOR LUNCH!

VERY WELL DONE! HELP ME WITH THE FISH.
NOW SALT THESE GUYS TO EAT THEM LATER.
YOU EAT THE REST, KALEV.
WAIT! KEEP THE GALLBLADDER, HEART, AND LIVER SEPARATE.
YEAH? WHAT ARE YOU GOING TO DO WITH THEM?
IT IS SAID THAT IF THE FISH'S HEART AND LIVER ARE BURNED IN FRONT OF A PERSON SUFFERING FROM AN EVIL SPIRIT, THROUGH PRAYER, THE EVIL SPIRIT WILL DISAPPEAR.

DEFEAT EVIL SPIRITS? WHAT ABOUT THE GALLBLADDER?
IF IN PRAYER, YOU APPLY GALLBLADDER TO THE EYES OF A PERSON WITH WHITE MEMBRANES AND BLOW ON THEM, THE EYES WILL HEAL.
THAT MIGHT HELP!
WOW! THANK YOU, LORD!

히이잉
HEE-HAW
IT'S BEEN A WHILE.
MY MOTHER SENT ME ON A TRIP, BUT MY HEART DOESN'T FEEL AT EASE AT ALL . . .
I HOPE GOD HEARS MY PRAYERS.
MAYBE I CAN PRAY BETTER BY THE WATER.
터억
NEIGH

WELL, WELL, WHAT A PRETTY SWEET GIRL!
쿠궁!
GRRRR
BANDITS!
AH, BOSS! THAT WOMAN!
속닥 속닥
WHISPER
WHY DO YOU CARE?
WELL, IT DOESN'T MATTER IF YOU SELL HER AS A SLAVE!
크크크
HAHAHA
WOW!
MASTER! LET'S HURRY BACK!

타다다
AHHHH!
NO, PUT ME DOWN!
WHAT A PAIN.
WOOSH
ARRR
BUT YOU CAN'T RUN AWAY FROM ME!
BROTHER, WE ARE ALMOST TO MEDIA, RIGHT?

YES, TOMORROW YOU WILL BE ABLE TO STAY AT THE HOUSE OF RAGUEL, YOUR RELATIVE WHO LIVES IN MEDIA.
타닥
CRACKLE
I HEARD THAT RAGUEL IS MY FATHER'S CLOSEST RELATIVE.
RIGHT, RAGUEL HAS ONLY ONE DAUGHTER, NAMED SARAH.
REALLY?
YOU ARE HIS CLOSEST RELATIVE, SO YOU ARE QUALIFIED TO MARRY HER!
WHOA, MARRY HER?
벌떡
RISE
A VERY WISE, BRAVE, AND VERY BEAUTIFUL WOMAN.

HER FATHER RAGUEL IS ALSO A GREAT PERSON.
IS THAT YOUR WAY OF SAYING THAT I SHOULD MARRY HIS DAUGHTER?
IT MAY SOUND A BIT STRANGE TO YOU, BUT . . .
GOD WANTS IT SO.
GOD WANTS IT . . . ?
짹 짹
TWEET TWEET

HELLO, ARE YOU PASSING THROUGH ECBATANA TOO?
THAT'S RIGHT.
YOU'RE LUCKY WE MET YOU.
WE RAN INTO BANDITS NEARBY AND MANAGED TO ESCAPE.
THIEVES?! LET'S GO AROUND ECBATANA AND GO THE OTHER WAY.
찌릿
HMMMMM
DON'T YOU BELIEVE ME, TOBY? NOTHING WILL HAPPEN TO US.

WE DON'T NEED TO GO TO RAGUEL'S HOUSE THAT BADLY.
?
RAGUEL, DID YOU JUST SAY RAGUEL?
!
YES, I AM A CLOSE RELATIVE, AND MY KINSMAN SAYS THAT I SHOULD MARRY HIS DAUGHTER.
WHAT ABOUT THE EVIL SPIRIT?
덜덜덜
TREMBLE
DO YOU REALLY WANT TO DIE?
WHY ARE YOU TALKING ABOUT DYING?

WELL, THERE'S A RUMOR GOING AROUND ABOUT HER . . .
SHE HAS ALREADY MARRIED SEVEN MEN, AND THEY ALL DIED IN THE BRIDAL CHAMBER.
WHEN A MAN GOES INTO THAT WOMAN'S ROOM, HE DIES THAT NIGHT!
IS THAT REALLY TRUE?
섬뜩
HUH?
RAGUEL HAS NO SON.
IT IS CLEAR THAT THE DEVIL IS AFTER THE WOMAN'S HUSBAND . . . IT MUST BE A CURSE!

BROTHER AZARIAH, DID YOU KNOW ABOUT THIS WHEN YOU ASKED ME TO MARRY SARAH?
. . .
I DID KNOW, TOBY!
IT MUST BE A PLOY TO TAKE EVERYTHING WHEN I DIE!
IT'S NOT LIKE THAT!
DON'T COME ANY CLOSER!
휙
SWAT
I CAN'T TRUST YOU ANYMORE. I'M GOING ON ALONE!
TOBY!
타다다다-
DASH

AH, THAT HILL!
NO! DON'T GO THERE!
IT'S A DANGEROUS PLACE WHERE BANDITS HIDE. TSK, TSK.
WELL . . .
UNBELIEVABLE!
헉헉-
PANT PANT
BROTHER AZARIAH ...

I REALLY TRUSTED AND FOLLOWED HIM LIKE A BIG BROTHER!
헉헉-
PANT PANT
HE MUST NOT GET TO MY FORTUNE!
으르르
GRRRR
멍멍
WOOF WOOF
WHY . . . !
WHAT... WHAT ABOUT FORTUNE?
쿠-궁
SURPRISE!

HAHAHA . . . YOU DIDN'T EVEN KNOW YOU CRAWLED INTO A TIGER'S DEN!
흐흐흐
HAHAHAHA
스릉
TING
AH!
GIVE US EVERYTHING YOU HAVE!
OF COURSE, IF YOU DON'T HAVE ANYTHING VALUABLE, YOU'RE WORTH NOTHING TO US!
SWOOSH
AFTER ALL THIS . . . NOW I'LL DIE ALONE!

퍽
THUNK!
AHHH!
WHO, WHO ARE YOU?
빠악
POW!
KAHHHH!
쿠당
CRASH!

OH NO!
DON'T JUST STAND THERE!
크으으으으
TREMBLE
HELP ME!
빠악
CRASH!
WHY DID YOU COME TO HELP ME?

퍼억
POP
퍼억
BAM
크릉
GRRR
왕
CHOMP
WHO'S NEXT?
턱
CLENCH
NOOOOO, AZARIAH!

KA-
BAM!
!
TOBY! LET'S RUN UP THERE!
YES!
CHOMP

탁!
타닥!
THUMP THUMP!
WHY IS IT SO NOISY?
PANT PANT
헉 헉
GASP!
챙-
CLUNK
EEK!
THERE!
콱
으악
AHHHHHHH
HUH?
HURRY! GET HIM!
퍽
WHACK

헉헉
GASP
COME ON OUT!
GA
GRASP
두근 두근
BA-DUM
BA-DUM
와!
HEY!
TOBY, WHAT ARE YOU DOING?
CAREFUL!

HUH?!
FIND YOU LATER!
쿠우우우—
HEHEHEH

촤아아아악
AHHHHHHH
NOOOO!
THESE MONSTERS!

RETREAT!
GREAT JOB, TOBY! YOU WERE GREAT!
SQUEEZE
WHY ARE YOU HELPING ME?
BECAUSE YOU ARE IN DANGER, OF COURSE!
BUT I DIDN'T TRUST YOU AND I STILL DON'T!

YOU LACK FAITH. YOUR FATHER IS A MAN OF GREAT FAITH.
STOP TALKING ABOUT THAT NONSENSE! MY FATHER BELIEVES IN GOD, NOT IN YOU!
I NEVER DID ANYTHING THAT WOULD HARM YOU. YOU WERE THE ONE WHO DOUBTED ME!
...
FINE! WHETHER YOU BELIEVE ME OR NOT, I WILL GO TO MEDIA TO KEEP MY PROMISE TO YOUR FATHER.

BELIEVE YOUR GUIDE, OR NOT, DO WHAT YOU LIKE!
SHEESH, HE WANTS ME TO TRUST HIM COMPLETELY!
WHERE DID THAT WOMAN GO?
두리번 두리번
WHIRL
?
WAIT FOR ME!
후다다-
THUMP THUMP

I'M GLAD THAT MAN WASN'T HURT SAVING ME.
BUT HE CAN'T HAVE YOU!
WHAT'S THAT? SOMEONE IS COMING!

MORE VICTIMS! I LOOK FORWARD TO IT.
낼름
SWIRL
낼름
SWIRL
IS THIS PLACE ECBATANA . . . ?

YES, BUT IF YOU DON'T WANT TO STAY AT RAGUEL'S HOUSE, WE WILL LOOK ELSEWHERE.
YOU SAID IT WAS GOD'S WILL THAT I MARRY RAGUEL'S DAUGHTER?
DO YOU WANT TO LISTEN TO GOD NOW?
흠
HMMM
MY FATHER TOLD ME I SHOULD GET MARRIED.
BECAUSE THAT IS THE TEACHING.
YOUR FATHER IS A MAN OF PRAYER.
BUT A DEMON IS OBSESSED WITH HER. I'M AFRAID!

SARAH IS BEAUTIFUL AND WOULD BE A WONDERFUL WIFE! IT IS THE EVIL SPIRIT, ASMODEUS.
SARAH NO LONGER HAS THE STRENGTH TO FIGHT THE EVIL SPIRIT, BUT SHE PRAYS TO GOD EVERY DAY.
SHE PRAYS, "I BEG YOU TO HURRY AND TAKE ME TO HEAVEN."
. . .
I WANT TO FIGHT THIS EVIL SPIRIT.
YOU HAVE THE COURAGE TO DO IT.

ARE YOU THERE?
똑똑똑
KNOCK KNOCK
WHO . . . ? YES, YOU ARE . . . ?
LONG TIME NO SEE, IT'S AZARIAH.
빙
SWISH
응~
YES
AH, YES, MY KINSMAN.
HAVE YOU TWO MET BEFORE?
NO.
오잉?
HMM?
EDNA, EDNA, A GUEST!

WELCOME! HAVE A GOOD REST IN OUR HOME!
. . . ?
멈칫
PAUSE
OH!
YOU! YOU!
아앗-!
WHAT?!
탁 탁
THUMP THUMP THUMP

BY THE WAY . . . WELL, WHO WAS AZARIAH?
비 잉
SWISH
OH, YES.
짝
CLAP
EDNA, DOESN'T THIS YOUNG FELLOW LOOK LIKE TOBIT?
YES, THEY REALLY DO LOOK ALIKE!
WHERE ARE YOU FROM, BROTHER?
I'M FROM NINEVEH.

THEN DO YOU KNOW A MAN NAMED TOBIT?
YES, HE IS MY FATHER.
WHAT!?
OH! TO SEE FAMILY AGAIN!
와락
SQUEEZE
PAT
YOUR FATHER REALLY IS OUR FAMILY'S PRIDE!

HEY, LET'S GET A RAM! WE HAVE A SPECIAL GUEST!
I HEARD THAT DEAR TOBIT WENT BLIND. WHAT A TERRIBLE THING.
OH TOBY! YOU'VE GROWN UP SO NICELY. WE HAD TO LEAVE OUR HOMETOWNS.
YES, EAT AND DRINK HAPPILY TODAY.
우하핫
HAHAHAHA
WHEN I WAS EXILED, I REALLY HAD NOTHING.
딸꾹
HICCUP
OH, HERE WE GO AGAIN!

BUT I WORKED HARD, AND NOW I AM RICH AND WELL-KNOWN IN ECBATANA.
YOUR FATHER HELPED US GREATLY. ANYTHING YOU NEED, PLEASE JUST ASK.
흠
HMMM
YES, I HAVE SOMETHING TO TELL YOU.
I HEARD ABOUT SARAH FROM OUR RELATIVE, AZARIAH.
UGH!

!
쿠
궁
GASP
OK, LET'S JUST DRINK, EAT, AND BE MERRY TONIGHT.
PLEASE, I WOULD LIKE TO TAKE SARAH AS MY WIFE.
WELL, THEN I DON'T HAVE THE RIGHT TO GIVE SARAH TO ANYONE ELSE.
끙
UMM...
척!
TELL HIM THE TRUTH SO HE LEAVES.
CLENCH

SARAH!
SEVEN HUSBANDS HAVE ALREADY DIED BECAUSE OF THE EVIL SPIRIT.
I KNOW!
YOU KNOW? AND YOU STILL WANT TO MARRY ME?
LET'S FACE THE EVIL SPIRIT WITH GOD. PLEASE!
THAT CAN'T BE DONE . . .
YOU CAN'T OBJECT. I HAVE A RIGHT TO MARRY SARAH!

I CAN'T HELP BUT SAY YES! COME CLOSE.
ACCORDING TO THE LAW OF MOSES, SARAH IS NOW YOUR WIFE.
SO YOU CAN TAKE IT TO YOUR FAMILY, TOBY . . .
휴우-
SIGH

I'LL DRAW THE MARRIAGE CONTRACT RIGHT NOW!
스윽-
SCRIBBLE
SARAH, ARE YOU OKAY? I AM NERVOUS TOO BECAUSE IT IS ALL SO SUDDEN.
부르르
TREMBLE
DEAR, LET'S BE BRAVE.

GOD WILL HEAR YOUR PRAYERS NOW. YOUR MOTHER BELIEVES THIS.
HEHEHE, HE'S FINALLY HERE, ANOTHER PREY OF MINE.
스르르
WOOSH

하하하
HAHAHHAHA
끼익
URRK
덜컥
CREAAAK
TOBY! WHY ME . . .
벌떡
RISE
THIS TIME I CAN HELP YOU.

DON'T ACT LIKE A FOOL. RUN AWAY NOW!
OF COURSE I AM AFRAID TOO, BUT NOW I FEEL WE CAN DEFEAT IT WITH GOD.
LET'S PRAY FOR GOD'S HELP AND PROTECTION.
WOOSH
WHAT ARE YOU TALKING ABOUT!?

DEAR GOD . . .
팟
POW
사 삭
SPRINKLE
슈우우우-
WHOOSH
깜짝
EWWWW
!

WHAT IS THAT SMELL?
스르르
AHH
쾅!
BANG
IT'S THE EVIL SPIRIT!
쾅!
BANG
으아아
쾅!
BANG
TOBIAS!
OH, I CAN'T STAND IT ANYMORE!
슈웅
AHHH!
퍽!
THUD
OUCH!

콰아아아아
CRASH
콰지직!
WHOOSH
IT'S YOU.
슈우우-
WHOOOSH
STOP THERE!
파앗
CLENCH

ARE YOU HURT?
NO, I'M OKAY.
THE DEMON HAS LEFT!
GOD HAS HELPED US.
HE HEARD MY PRAYERS AND SENT YOU.
꼬옥
GRASP
LET'S SAY A PRAYER OF THANKS!

슈우우우-
WHOOOSH
훼이-
TREMBLE
NO, YOU'RE TAKING ME AWAY FROM THAT WOMAN.
DON'T EVEN DREAM OF GOING BACK!
YOU, WHO ARE YOU AGAIN?

WAIT!
쿠앙!
SHINE!
!
OOPS
쿠궁-
CRASH
CRUMBLE
YOUR TRICKS WON'T WORK ON ME!
퍽
BAM
STOP RESISTING!

HE IS STRONG TO TAKE ASMODEUS LIKE THIS!
CRUMBLE
WHO ARE YOU?
OUCH
THERE IS NO ONE WHO CAN STAND UP AGAINST ME!
슈우우우우
AHHHHHH
팟ー
POW
HE HAS SENT ME TO JUDGE YOU.
NO WAY!

WICKED ONE, BE JUDGED BY THE LIGHT OF GOD!
처억
CLENCH
NO, I HATE IT! DON'T DO IT!
번쩍-
SHINE
으아아
AHHHHH
ONE MISSION COMPLETE!
THE NEXT DAY

THAT STUPID BOY, TOBY! I TRIED TO TELL HIM.
RAGUEL, DID YOU JUST COME FROM DIGGING A GRAVE?
I DON'T WANT TO BE RIDICULED ANY LONGER.
HOW WILL I TELL TOBIT . . .
YOU CAN GO CHECK TO SEE IF THE GROOM LIVES.
USELESS! HE CAN'T STILL BE ALIVE.

HE WAS A GOOD-LOOKING KID . . .
THE GROOM IS SLEEPING!
YES, I WILL GO BURY HIM!
휴우
PHEW
WAIT, WHAT?
!
HE IS SLEEPING . . . ?
YOU MUST BE WRONG. NO? ARE YOU SURE?
HE WAS SNORING . . .

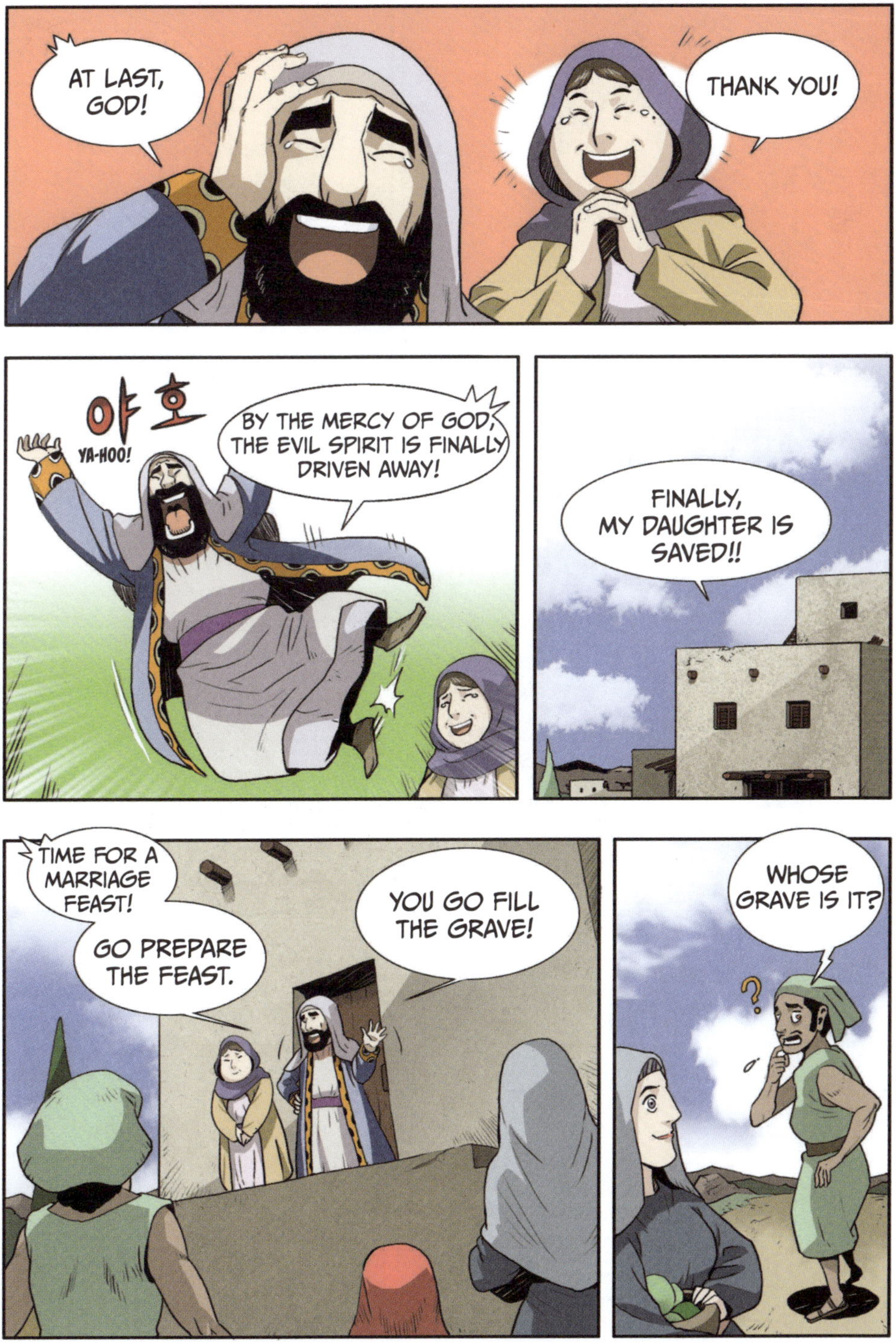

AT LAST, GOD!
THANK YOU!
야호
YA-HOO!
BY THE MERCY OF GOD, THE EVIL SPIRIT IS FINALLY DRIVEN AWAY!
FINALLY, MY DAUGHTER IS SAVED!!
TIME FOR A MARRIAGE FEAST!
GO PREPARE THE FEAST.
YOU GO FILL THE GRAVE!
WHOSE GRAVE IS IT?

우 하하하 -
HAHAHAHAHA
OH CHILDREN! NOW YOU WILL FEAST WITH ME FOR FOURTEEN DAYS!
AND YOU, MY SON, NOW EVERYTHING I HAVE IS YOURS!
부비
PAT
부비
PAT
꼬옥
SQUEEZE

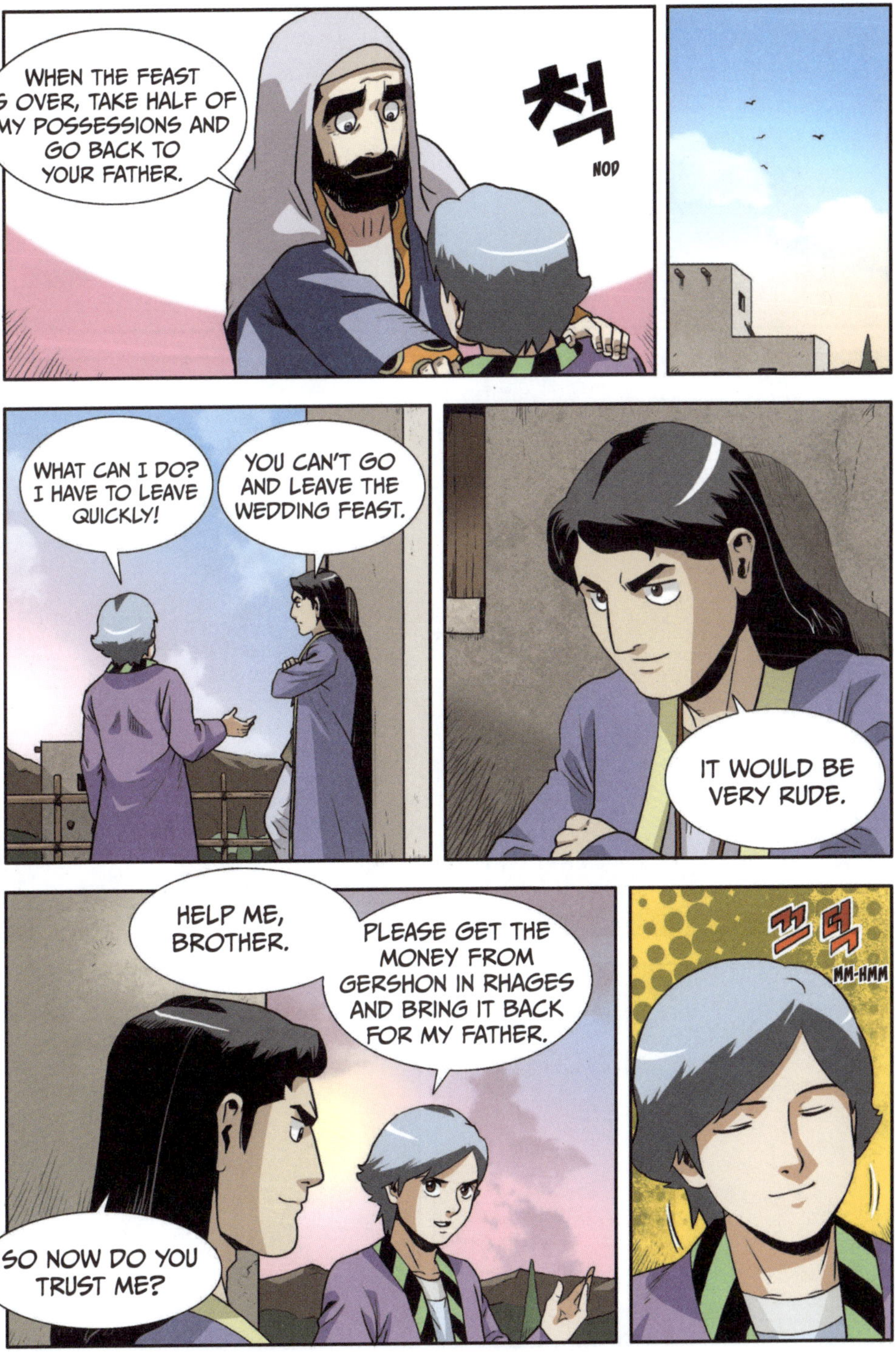
WHEN THE FEAST IS OVER, TAKE HALF OF MY POSSESSIONS AND GO BACK TO YOUR FATHER.
척
NOD
WHAT CAN I DO? I HAVE TO LEAVE QUICKLY!
YOU CAN'T GO AND LEAVE THE WEDDING FEAST.
IT WOULD BE VERY RUDE.
HELP ME, BROTHER.
PLEASE GET THE MONEY FROM GERSHON IN RHAGES AND BRING IT BACK FOR MY FATHER.
SO NOW DO YOU TRUST ME?
끄덕
MM-HMM

OKAY, YOUR FATHER IS WAITING FOR YOU TO COME BACK. I WILL GO SO THERE IS NO DELAY.
THANK YOU. I CAN'T WAIT FOR MY FATHER TO SEE AGAIN.
WHY HAVEN'T THEY CONTACTED ME YET? COULD IT BE THAT GERSHON IS ALREADY DEAD AND THERE IS NO WAY TO RETURN THE MONEY?
안절부절
WHERE ARE THEY?
TOBIAS IS PROBABLY DEAD.
ANNA, WHAT ARE YOU TALKING ABOUT!?
깜짝
GASP!

THERE MUST BE LOTS OF BANDITS. HE HAS ALREADY LEFT THIS WORLD.
엉 엉 엉
SOB
CRYING IS USELESS! HE'LL BE FINE!
OH, MY DEAR CHILD! I DIDN'T WANT TO SEND YOU AWAY!
OH, ANNA! THE YOUNG MAN WHO LEFT WITH HIM IS RELIABLE! HE WILL BE FINE.
HOW DO YOU KNOW THAT!? I CAN'T LIVE WITHOUT HIM!
. . . !
버럭
AHHH!
푸욱
SLUMP
TOBY . . .

HE SHOULD BE BACK TODAY . . .
!
WOW, YOU'RE BACK!
ARE YOU TOBIAS? YOU LOOK SO MUCH LIKE TOBIT!
SORRY I'M LATE. I HAD TO BRING THIS PERSON TO THE CELEBRATION.
처억-
TA-DA
I AM GERSHON, THE ONE WHO HELD ON TO THE MONEY.

MAY GOD BLESS TOBIAS' WIFE, FATHER-IN-LAW, AND MOTHER-IN-LAW.
THANK YOU!
THE WEDDING FEAST CONTINUED FOR FOURTEEN DAYS.
우하하
HAHAHAHAHA
PLEASE SEND ME TO MY FATHER NOW.
벌떡
AHEM
STAY A LITTLE LONGER. SOON YOU BOTH WILL BE GONE . . .
BUT I CAN'T DELAY ANY LONGER. I AM THINKING OF MY WORRIED FATHER.

흑!
SNIFFLE
IF YOU MUST, THEN GO. AS PROMISED, TAKE HALF OF MY POSSESSIONS WITH YOU.
WE'LL LEAVE TOMORROW MORNING.
짹 짹
TWEET TWEET
철컹 - 철컹
CLUNK-CLUNK
TAKE CARE! MAY YOU ALWAYS BE HAPPY!
THANK YOU. WE WILL DEFINITELY COME BACK.

MANY BLESSINGS, SARAH!
THE WAY BACK DIDN'T TAKE VERY LONG.
OH, TOBY . . .
다다닷 –
PIT-PAT
WOOF WOOF

OH MY,
KALEV!!
IT CAN'T BE!
MOTHER!
처억
CLIP CLOP

YES, IT'S TOBY!!
WHAT, TOBY? IS TOBIAS HERE?
MY SON IS BACK, TOBY, TOBY!
OH! GOD PROTECTED YOU! THANK YOU!
스윽
SQUEEZE
FATHER!
HAVE FAITH, TOBY!

탁탁-
RUSTLE
TOBY, WHAT ARE YOU DOING?
사악
SPRINKLE
휘이
WHOOSH
!
번쩍
GASP

MY EYES ARE CLEAR!
GOD HEALED THEM!
OH, I DON'T KNOW WHAT YOU HAVE BEEN THROUGH ON YOUR TRIP.
THANK YOU, GOD. YOU HEARD MY PRAYERS, LORD.
YES, IT'S SO AMAZING!
THERE IS ANOTHER SURPRISE! I HAVE SOMEONE TO INTRODUCE.

SARAH, SAY HELLO TO YOUR PARENTS.
FATHER, I AM SARAH, DAUGHTER OF RAGUEL.
WHAT! RAGUEL'S DAUGHTER!
아하하
HAHA
TODAY I AM THE HAPPIEST PERSON IN THE WORLD!

TOBY! I GUESS MY JOB IS DONE NOW.
ARE YOU LEAVING ALREADY? THE PARTY IS ABOUT TO BEGIN.
I HAVE SEEN ENOUGH HAPPINESS. I MUST LEAVE.
I HAVE LEARNED A LOT FROM YOU, BROTHER AZARIAH. LET ME TALK TO MY FATHER FOR A MOMENT.
ALL THE JEWS HERE IN NINEVEH ARE REJOICING FOR YOU!
SPARKLE
I'M GLAD THAT MY SON HAS RETURNED SAFELY. IT'S LIKE A DREAM TO SEE HIM WITH MY OWN EYES, AND MY PRETTY DAUGHTER-IN-LAW BESIDE HIM.

FATHER, AZARIAH SAID HE IS LEAVING.
REALLY? BE GENEROUS TO HIM. THIS IS ALL BECAUSE GOD SENT HIS HELP.
YES, WITHOUT HIS HELP, WE WOULD NOT HAVE BEEN ABLE TO RETURN SAFELY.
I'M THINKING OF GIVING HIM HALF OF THE SILVER. WHAT DO YOU THINK?
UM . . . BEFORE I LEAVE, I HAVE SOMETHING TO TELL YOU TWO.

TOBY, I HAVE NO NEED FOR YOUR SILVER.
GOD ALREADY KNOWS HOW YOU WILL HELP YOUR NEIGHBORS WITH IT.
NO NEED . . . WHO ARE YOU?
샤악-
SWOOSH
ALL OF THIS IS GOD'S WILL. I JUST FOLLOW HIM!
슈우우우-
SHINE

넙죽!
BOW
NO!!!
GOD HEARD YOUR PRAYERS AND DECIDED TO HELP YOU.
덜덜덜
TREMBLE
YOU HAVE BEEN FAITHFUL.
GOD IS PLEASED WITH YOU.
SO, CONTINUE TO LIVE IN PRAISE OF THE LORD, WITHOUT CHANGING.

WHAT ARE YOU?
덜덜덜
TREMBLE
I AM RAPHAEL, ONE OF THE SEVEN ARCHANGELS.
TOBIAS, IT WAS A PLEASANT TRIP.
팟-
SWIRL
...!
멍~
WHAT?!
AZARIAH WAS AN ARCHANGEL!

TOBY, YOU MUST HAVE LEARNED A VERY VALUABLE LESSON FROM THIS TRIP!
GOD ALWAYS SHOWS MERCY TO THOSE WHO SEEK IT.
HE WILL BRING YOU OUT OF DREADFUL RUIN.

TOBIAS AND SARAH WERE JOYFUL AND HAD A HAPPY FAMILY.

TOBIT LIVED RESPECTFULLY IN NINEVEH AND DIED PEACEFULLY.
EVEN AFTER HE REGAINED HIS SIGHT, HE GAVE ALMS.
HE LIVED HAPPILY ACCORDING TO GOD'S WILL.
WHEN TOBIAS' MOTHER DIED, HE BURIED HER NEXT TO HIS FATHER.

ACCORDING TO HIS FATHER'S WILL, TOBIAS LIVED WITH HIS FATHER-IN-LAW, RAGUEL, IN ECBATANA IN MEDIA.
HE ALSO INHERITED HIS FATHER-IN-LAW'S FORTUNE AND LIVED WITH WEALTH AND HONOR UNTIL THE AGE OF ONE HUNDRED AND SEVENTEEN.
NINEVEH, THE PLACE HIS FATHER CALLED "A PLACE FULL OF INJUSTICE," WAS DESTROYED. BY FOLLOWING HIS FATHER'S WILL, TOBIAS' FAMILY MANAGED TO ESCAPE.
IT IS SAID THAT TOBIAS PRAISED THE ETERNAL LORD OUR GOD HIS WHOLE LIFE.

Prayer to Saint Raphael

Saint Raphael, God sent you to guide and assist Tobias throughout his travels. Please help me as I journey through each day. Protect me from any dangers I face on my own path to holiness. Guide me toward others who love God. As you healed Tobit and Sarah through God's grace, heal me of all my physical and spiritual illnesses. I especially ask *(mention your own intentions here)*. Amen.

Saint Raphael is the patron saint of travelers, health care workers, the blind, and those who are looking for a spouse. He is one of the three archangels named in Scripture, along with Saint Michael and Saint Gabriel. The feast day of the archangels is on September 29.